WAR PLANES

Radar Jammers:
The EA-6B Prowlers
by Bill Sweetman

DISCARD

CAPSTONE
HIGH-INTEREST
BOOKS

an imprint of Capstone Press
Mankato, Minnesota

Capstone High-Interest Books are published by Capstone Press
151 Good Counsel Drive, P.O. Box 669, Mankato, Minnesota 56002
http://www.capstone-press.com

Library of Congress Cataloging-in-Publication Data
Sweetman, Bill.
    Radar jammers: the EA-6B Prowlers / by Bill Sweetman.
    p. cm.—(War Planes)
    Includes bibliographical references and index.
    Summary: Introduces the EA-6B Prowlers, their missions, equipment,
and use in the military as radar jamming escorts to other aircraft.
    ISBN 0-7368-1069-2
    1. EA-6 (Electronic warfare aircraft)—Juvenile literature. 2. Radar—
Interference—Juvenile literature. [1. EA-6 (Electronic warfare aircraft)
2. Radar—Interference.] I. Title. II. War planes.
UG1242.E43 S94 2002
623.7'46—dc21   2001003637

**Special thanks to Lt. Kenneth F. Setser of the U.S. Navy for his help in
preparing this book.**

Editorial Credits
Matt Doeden, editor; Timothy Halldin, cover and interior designer;
    Katy Kudela, photo researcher

Photo Credits
Defense Visual Information Center, 6
Ted Carlson/Fotodynamics, cover, 9, 10, 13, 16–17, 18, 21, 22, 28
U.S. Navy photo, 1, 4, 24, 27

1 2 3 4 5 6 07 06 05 04 03 02

Table of Contents

Chapter One

Learn About

- Prowler missions
- Electronic countermeasures
- Prowlers in combat

The EA-6B in Action

Four U.S. Air Force F-16 fighters fly more than 20,000 feet (6,100 meters) above the ground. The pilots fly the planes over enemy territory toward an enemy base. A fifth plane flies 5 miles (8 kilometers) from the F-16s. It is an EA-6B Prowler.

Ahead, enemy troops at a surface-to-air missile (SAM) site watch the fighter planes on radar. The enemy troops prepare to shoot missiles at the planes. The SAM crew waits for the fighters to move within missile range.

Crew members locate targets on special screens.

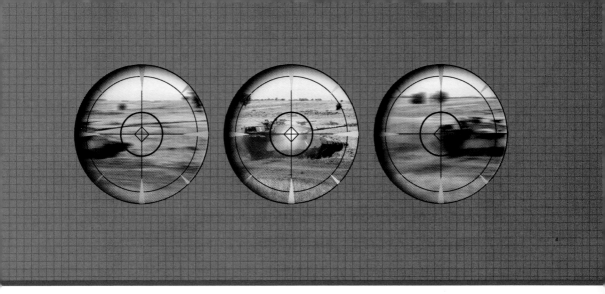

Crew members aboard the Prowler know about the SAM site. They studied maps and photos of the area before the mission. They can see the exact location of the enemy radar station on special screens. The crew members use a powerful transmitter to send out strong radio signals. The crew members point the signals at the enemy radar station.

Suddenly, the enemy radar screens show a bright patch of white. The SAM crew can no longer see the fighter planes. Without radar, the enemy troops cannot fire missiles at the fighters.

Soon, the fighters speed over the SAM site. The planes are safe. The Prowler's crew has performed its mission by jamming the enemy's radar.

About the Prowler

The Prowler is an unusual military aircraft. It does not rely on powerful guns and missiles. Instead, it carries special radio equipment. Prowler crew members protect troops and aircraft by preventing enemy radar from working properly. The Prowler's main mission is called electronic countermeasures. A countermeasure is a device used to interrupt a sensing mechanism such as radar.

The Northrop Grumman Aerospace Corporation built the Prowler in the 1960s. The Prowler's first test flight occurred on May 25, 1968. The plane entered Navy service in July 1971. Today, the Navy has 120 Prowlers.

The Prowler remains one of the Navy's most useful aircraft. Prowler pilots flew with fighter pilots when the U.S. military attacked Serbia's military in 1999. Most fighter missions included at least one Prowler.

The Prowler has been in service more than 30 years.

Learn About

- The A-6 Intruder
- Prowler engines
- AN/ALQ-99 Tactical Jamming System

Inside the EA-6B

The Prowler's design was based on another U.S. aircraft called the A-6 Intruder. The U.S. Navy and Marine Corps used this attack bomber during the Vietnam War (1954–1975). The Navy also used a later model of the Intruder called the A-6E in the Gulf War (1991). The Navy stopped using the Intruder in the late 1990s.

Body and Engines

The Prowler is a large, durable airplane. It can weigh as much as 61,500 pounds (27,450 kilograms) when fully loaded. Thick wings hold most of the airplane's fuel. Large hinged flaps on the wings provide extra lift for takeoffs and landings. The Prowler's wings also can fold up. The Prowler often takes off from and lands on aircraft carriers. Its folded wings take up less space on a carrier's deck.

Two Pratt & Whitney J52-P408A engines power the Prowler. Each engine produces 10,400 pounds (4,717 kilograms) of thrust. This force pushes the airplane through the air. The Prowler can reach speeds of 575 miles (920 kilometers) per hour. It has a range of about 1,150 miles (1,840 kilometers). The range is the distance an aircraft can travel without refueling.

The Prowler can fold its wings to save space.

Payload

The Prowler carries weapons and equipment in wing stations mounted under the plane. Each Prowler has five wing stations. These stations also are called pods. Each pod holds radar jamming equipment, a missile, or a fuel tank. The equipment a Prowler carries on a mission is called the payload.

Prowler pods usually carry radar jamming transmitters. These devices send out signals that block enemy radar. Each transmitter is part of the AN/ALQ-99 Tactical Jamming System. This system includes all of the radar jamming equipment aboard a Prowler.

The Prowler's radar transmitters are very powerful. The radio waves they produce are so strong that they could harm the crew. The airplane's cockpit is covered in a thin layer of metal. The metal reflects radio waves away from the crew.

Pilot Controls

The Prowler has many controls and gauges inside its cockpit. The pilot uses the controls

EA-6B Specifications

Function:	Electronic countermeasures
Manufacturer:	Northrop Grumman Aerospace Corporation
Date Deployed:	July 1971
Length:	59 feet, 10 inches (17.7 meters)
Wingspan:	53 feet (15.9 meters)
Height:	16 feet, 8 inches (4.9 meters)
Max. Weight:	61,500 pounds (27,450 kilograms)
Engine:	Two Pratt & Whitney J52-P408A engines
Thrust:	10,400 pounds (4,717 kilograms) per engine
Speed:	575 miles (920 kilometers) per hour
Ceiling:	37,600 feet (11,460 meters)
Range:	1,150 miles (1,840 kilometers)
Crew:	Four (one pilot and three electronic countermeasures officers)

to fly the plane. The pilot uses gauges to keep track of the plane's speed, location, and fuel supply.

Prowler pilots' main controls are the control stick and the throttle. Pilots steer their planes with the control stick. Pilots use the throttle to control their planes' speed. Many controls and buttons are located on the stick and throttle.

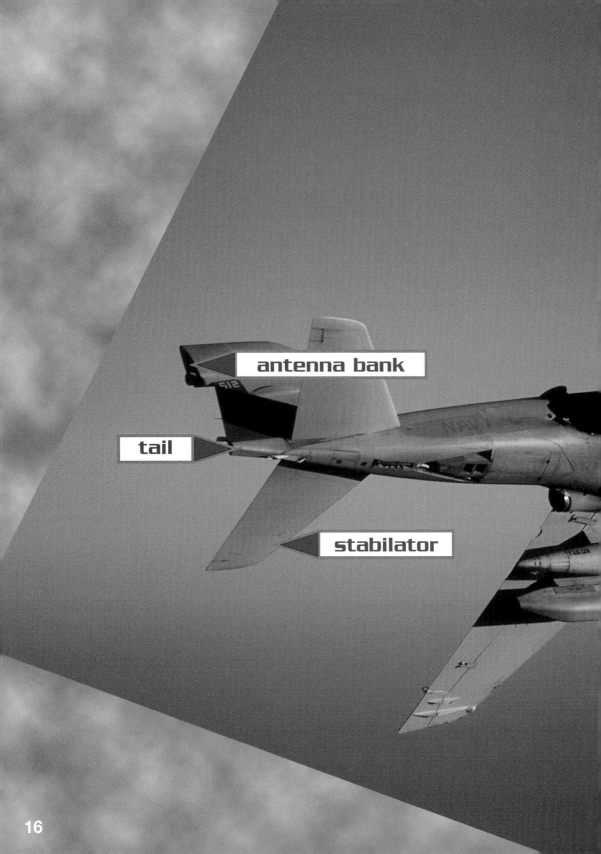

antenna bank

tail

stabilator

The EA-6B Prowler

AGM-88 HARM missile

refueling probe

fuel tank

radar transmitter

Chapter Three

Learn About

- Radar jamming
- Electronic countermeasures officers
- The HARM missile

Weapons and Tactics

The Prowler is not a fighter aircraft. It does not carry weapons to fight against enemy fighter planes. It does not carry powerful bombs. Instead, Prowler crew members prevent enemies from easily targeting U.S. troops and aircraft. Prowler crew members use strong radio signals to jam enemy radar.

Radar Jamming

Radar jamming equipment transmits strong radio signals at enemy radar stations. These radar stations use radio waves to detect aircraft. The waves bounce off aircraft. The radar stations detect the bounced waves. Radar jammers send out signals that are stronger than the normal radar signals. Radar jamming signals prevent radar stations from receiving bounced signals.

Each Prowler includes four crew members. The pilot flies the airplane. The other three crew members operate radar jamming equipment. They are called electronic countermeasures officers (ECMOs).

The Prowler's crew must prepare before a mission. Crew members must know where enemy radar stations are located. They look at maps and study photos taken from space to find enemy radar stations.

In the air, the crew searches for enemy radar signals. A computer aboard the plane reads the signals. The crew then uses the plane's transmitter to send out the jamming signals.

ECMOs operate the radar jamming equipment.

Prowlers may carry HARM missiles under the wings.

AGM-88A HARM

The Prowler does not carry many weapons. But it does carry the AGM-88A HARM missile. The HARM is an air-to-ground missile. This missile is designed to destroy radar stations.

The HARM is a guided missile. It includes an antenna to detect radar signals. The missile's guidance system uses these signals to steer the missile to a radar station. The missile's nose holds a 150-pound (68-kilogram) warhead. This explosive is designed to destroy the radar station it hits.

The HARM is 13 feet, 8 inches (4.1 meters) long. It weighs 800 pounds (360 kilograms). It travels 760 miles (1,216 kilometers) per hour or faster. Pilots can fire the HARM at targets more than 80 miles (129 kilometers) away.

HARM missiles do not always hit their targets. Enemies may see the HARM coming. They may then turn off their radar. The HARM then cannot steer itself toward the station. But the enemy cannot fire any missiles until the radar is turned on again.